In These Shoes

Poetry, Prose and Perceptions

from the pen of a sage

Brenda Stevenson

In These Shoes

Poetry, Prose and Perceptions
from the pen of a sage

Brenda R. Stevenson

In These Shoes
Poetry, Prose and Perceptions from the pen of a sage

ISBN: 978-1-7320704-5-5
All Rights Reserved.

Copyright © 2023 by Brenda R. Stevenson

No part of this book may be reproduced or transmitted in any form or by any means, graphic, electronic, or mechanical, including photocopying, recording, taping or by any information storage or retrieval system, without the permission in writing from the author or publisher.

Unless otherwise indicated, all scripture quotations are from the King James Version of the Bible.

Published by:
Ronnie J. Wells Publishing
P.O. Box 90151
Atlanta, Georgia 30364
adonai314@yahoo.com
(678) 416-8325

Cover Art by: Phanazz Concepts
(404) 579-8019

Printed in the United States of America.
All Rights Reserved under International Copyright Law.

TABLE OF CONTENTS

TABLE OF CONTENTS

DEDICATION

With heartfelt love and admiration, I dedicate this collection of our mother's poetry, prose, and perceptions to the cherished memory of my beloved sisters, Melba J Renfro and Donna Renfro Lawson. The mark they made on my life will never be erased. May their spirits live on through the pages of this book and inspire others to embrace the beauty and uplifting power of words. - Venis L. Sims

INTRODUCTION

Get ready to embark on an incredible journey of faith, hope, and love as you step into Brenda R. Stevenson's world of poetry in her debut novel, In These Shoes. With powerful pieces such as I'm Not What I Use To Be, Another Leaf, Just Blessed, and The Hug, this collection of poetry is filled with life-changing words that will leave you feeling empowered and inspired.

Through Stevenson's intimate relationship with God, she shares her heart and offers guidance to those who may feel lost or alone in this world. With wisdom to help overcome everyday challenges and the reminder that our lives are on loan from God, this book of poetry is a true testament to the power of faith.

Life may not always be easy, but as you read In These Shoes, you'll discover how to find peace even in the midst of chaos. Whether you're experiencing frustration, anger, or doubt, Stevenson's words will uplift your spirits and remind you to be a prisoner of hope.

So, lace up your shoes and get ready to walk through life with renewed faith and inspiration.

CHAPTER 1

THE FOUNDATION

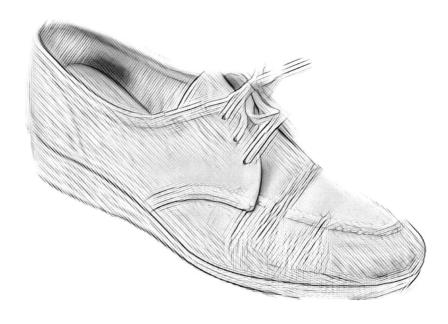

*"I've worn lots of shoes. I bet if I think about it really hard,
I could remember my first pair of shoes."*
Forrest Gump

ON LOAN FROM GOD

Thank you, Lord, for lending me A new house;
the one I share with my loving spouse.

It's pretty and neat with lots of space,
and within it I've found my special place.

From drafting table to completed construction
our house is now home.
Although we know it's really on loan!

When we speak of our home, there is no guessing,
We know without a doubt, it's another blessing!

The cat walks about suspicious and sniffing,
checking out the new quarters in which we are living.

The cat is in awe and so are we. Thanks again Dear Lord,
from my spouse, the cat and me.

"I believe that life is a journey, often difficult and sometimes incredibly cruel, but we are well equipped for it if only we tap into our talents and gifts and allow them to blossom."

LES BROWN

I'M A PRISONER OF HOPE

Lock me up. I'm a prisoner of hope!

Hope for a brighter day in my life.
Hope to be a better person each day of my life.

Hope to encourage the downtrodden
with a prayer to lift them up.
Hope to bridge the divide among us.
Hope to increase the compassion, love and
caring between us.

My greatest hope is to continue to keep the faith,
love, and trust in our sustainer God!

The list of hope is endless!

Won't you join me as a prisoner of hope?
Hope brought to fruition will yield amazing results!

*"If all difficulties were known at the outset of a long journey,
most of us would never start out at all."*

DAN RATHER

THE HUG

A hug is silent, yet says you care.
It says have confidence if you dare.

A hug is very verbal and says I understand.
I want to be a friend. I extend my helping hand.

A hug says that it will be okay,
As you travel along day by day.

A hug says let God abide,
His grace and mercy is always supplied.

A hug says the Comforter will come
and bind you in His love.
He watches over you from Heaven above.

Hug someone today.
Lift them in prayer and be on your way.

Trust the Master, your soul will sing.
Your blessings will be many for you've done the right thing!

"If you can't fly, then run.
If you can't walk run, then walk.
If you can't walk, then crawl.
But by all means keep moving."

MARTIN LUTHER KING, JR.

YOU KNOW THAT I KNOW

You know that I know this house is the shelter
you have provided me Lord.

A first-time owner and overjoyed with happiness,
You, Oh Lord, are My First Guest!

I welcome you during the day and throughout the night.
Help yourself to whatever you see.

Bless your Holy Name. You gave it all to me!

Order my steps and keep me on track,
that as I prosper Dear Lord, I will give something back.

"Faith and prayer are the vitamins of the soul; man cannot live in health without them."

MAHALIA JACKSON

THANKFUL

The sun came up to brighten my day.
After a good night's sleep the Lord started me on my way.
I'm thankful.

My body intact and free of pain.
God is good and always the same.
I'm thankful.

God's grace and mercy is more than enough for me.
He provides everything that I need.
I'm thankful.

Peace, joy, and contentment in my life,
displace sorrow, misery, and strife.
I'm thankful.

Thankful, thankful, thankful as can be.
I believe and have faith that God has His hand on me.

I'm thankful.

"Keep going. Your hardest times often lead to the greatest moments of your life. Keep going. Tough situations build strong People in the end."

ROY T. BENNETT

DID YOU REMEMBER?

Did you remember to thank God for watching over you
while you slept and slumbered?

Did you remember to thank God for touching you with his
finger of love and waking you to see a new day?

Did you remember to thank God for food,
shelter, and clothing?

Did you remember to thank God for a quiet,
non-violent neighborhood?

Did you remember to thank God for keeping you safe
and out of harm's way?

Did you remember to thank God for providing
your every need?

REMEMBER to thank God every day!
He is your saving grace!

"The smallest seed of faith is better than the largest fruit of happiness."

HENRY DAVID THOREAU

CHAPTER 2

THE TRANSITIONS

*"If you don't think shoes are important, just ask
Dorothy and Cinderella."*
Author Unknown

22

TO WASTE A MIND

To waste a mind is a terrible thing.
A mind can be a blank tablet,
or a slate consumed with beautiful images and words,
or a page filled with nonsense and evil thoughts,
twisted and cluttered without a doubt.

Don't waste your mind by letting it be a terrible thing.

Instead take the positive route,
and your mind will absorb all that abounds,
then, only storing what may never be found.

Behold the beauty of life as your being is touched
by the love that exudes from the heart and soul.
Make love and kindness your daily goal.

Thank you Oh Lord for the mind
I cannot see, smell or touch.
I promise not to waste it again.
Thank you so much.

*"All I have seen teaches me to trust the Creator
For all I have not seen."*

RALPH WALDO EMERSON

ANOTHER LEAF

Another leaf has fallen from your family tree of life,
and slipped quietly away…
their soul crossing over to be with God I pray.

Leaving loved ones behind to feel the pain of your absence,
yet understanding you had to go,
for God had summoned your presence!

Grieve if you must as all mortals do.
Let them flow as tears of joy
as you realize more everyday
there is no failure in the Lord.

God called your loved one from labor to rest.
Yes, I know, you loved this precious one so,
it is hard to let go.

Just try to remember God knows best!

*"The reason birds can fly and we can't is simply because
they have perfect faith,
for to have faith is to have wings."*

J.M. BARRIE

WORDS

Words don't come easy at a time like this.
Sorrow and sadness never seem to fit.

Death is an activity few want to own.
Yet, we know someday we will all be called to our
heavenly home.

From a distance I reach out with my long arms of love,
to comfort you by saying . . .

I pray your loved one abides with God up above.

"If you lose faith, you lose all."

Eleanor Roosevelt

LIFE IS A JOURNEY

Although life is a precious gift,
It's also a journey.

No matter how carefully you
Take each step, you will stumble.

Or even fall, and
It may not be your fault at all.

Just know your help is on the way.
Call Jesus. He is your mainstay.

He will pick you up and dust you off,
and give you strength to bear your cross.

"If you have a good support system like your family and your friends around you, then you can't go wrong. So just believe in yourself, do your thing, and stay strong in what you believe in."

Roman Reigns

HOP LIKE A BUNNY

There is always someone to try to steal your thunder!
Impossible, my friend, because you are the boom
that triggers the flash;
that ignites the bolt of electricity;
which kindles the spark of the flame;
that turns into the blaze which becomes the sweeping rage
intended to consume all that you've upstaged.

The old adage "Put your best foot forward"
does not apply to people of color.
We must put both feet together and 'hop like a bunny'
just to maintain our status quo.

I say to you "keep on hopping"
to show those that cause you pain;
that after the thunder and lightning
comes the refreshing rain

to wash away the filthy stain of hatred
and prove how their devious efforts were all done in vain;
as their evil plots against you suddenly go down the drain!

"We need never shout across the spaces to an absent God. He is nearer than our own soul, closer than our most secret thoughts."

A.W. Tozer

A FRIEND'S RESPONSE TO ALBINO BOY (VOICE OF A CHILD)

I see beneath the cover; there's more to you than skin,
a sweet and humble being who wants to be my friend.

The "cocky' attitude that you project today
is fake and only used to scare troublemakers away!

I know you've been mistreated and that's not really fair.
But, I just hope you know, how much I really care.

Chapter 3

THE MISCONCEPTION

"Momma said they'd take me anywhere..."
Forrest Gump

MISUNDERSTOOD

Sometimes I try so hard to be a loving guide,
through kind words, deeds, and concern.
Then I find I can't bridge the gap,
it's a hard lesson to learn.

The gap is much too much, and so I cry.

Misunderstood are my efforts as they abound.
In shock, accusations, and malice erupt from
volcanic-like mothers of others,
my face becomes distorted with a frown.

Tears flow, hurt is felt. I think I'm going to die.
I cry, I cry, I cry.

Oh Lord, I think again…misunderstood I have failed.
Evil engulfs my being, the devil emerges from hell!
I fight to keep from being consumed.

I pray for strength to carry on,
while all the time wondering what did I do wrong?

MISUNDERSTOOD
(continued)

I dry my tears and think,
Although by man I'm often misunderstood.
God will fix it. He is so good!

I pray God's mercy for those who cause me pain.
and for myself that I will not be guilty of the same.

"And having your feet shod with the gospel of peace."

Ephesians 6:15

TEARS

These tears are mine to shed,
they come from thoughts within my head.

As the tears flow like a raging river,
forcing open the floodgates
that are the windows of my soul.

The saltwater tries to drown my spirit
as my thoughts unfold.

Emotions run rampant, leaving me sometimes
high, and sometimes low,
similar to a tidal wave,
swift and treacherous day by day.

My cross, my cross, is so heavy to bear.
The load is lightened only by the angels of one who cares

Faith is the answer to keep my spirit alive.
I call on the Master to let me survive.

TEARS
(continued)

All my burdens I lay at his feet
And ask in prayer, my soul to keep.

Now calmed by His love and grace.
Tears of joy trickle down my face.

Peace! Yes, I have the peace of knowing it is clear.
No matter where I am, the Lord is near.

"But Without faith, it is impossible to please him, for he who comes to God must believe that He is and that He is a rewarder of them that diligently seek him."

Hebrews 11:6

LOOKS CAN BE DECEIVING

This body, the safebox of my soul,
appears intact and well-nourished,
as the heart pumps the fluid
of life to every cell within it.

Not so my friend its intelligence center,
the brain, is physically malfunctioning,
the room is spinning.

My balance is off and
I feel as if I've been hit with a stick.

The shooting pain within my brain
comes and leaves quickly like a thief in the night.
Zapping my energy as I struggle and fight.

I want to do more than maintain the status quo.
I want to feel good and be on the move.
There is so much to do.
I need to go, go, go!

LOOKS CAN BE DECEIVING
(continued)

No manmade plan or strategy will change this condition,
but I know God will bring it to fruition.

I give Him the praise that I can still pray and think,
for this ability could disappear in a wink!

*"For as the body without the spirit is dead,
so faith without works is dead also."*

James 2.26

I'M NOT WHAT I USE TO BE

I'm not what I used to be: Thank God for that.
I used to fuss, cuss and cry at the drop of a hat!

I'm older and wiser; foolish things are in the past.
It takes longer to do tasks once done in a flash!

Movement is slower; my step lost some pep;
but I'm okay with that,
There are still so many things I can do for myself!

I am grateful to have all of my faculties,
and to be able to take care of my personal needs.

My eyesight is dim, and my hearing is dull,
but I'm not incapacitated:
For this I am thankful and truly elated!

Though there are still scales to be removed from my eyes,
as the changes come, I accept whatever betides.
God is good and He always has been.
I trust Him more now than I did 'back when'!

I'M NOT WHAT I USE TO BE
(continued)

Getting old is a challenge, needless to say,
to avoid it one must die young anyway.

Well, it's too late for that and life has more to give,
So, Praise God and just LIVE, LIVE, LIVE!

"Now faith is the substance of things hoped for and the evidence of things not seen."

Hebrews 11.1

YESTERDAY

Yesterday I felt burdened down.
I walked around with an invisible frown.

The tribulations that abound had my head spinning.
It seemed around and around.

I prayed…had a short conversation with the Lord.
I told Him my troubles:
the ones I thought were too heavy to bear.
I envisioned His smile and imagined He said,
"Thanks for talking to me because I really care."

You know He said,
"You mortals will experience some strife.
That's a part of living. That's a part of life."

Today, I look up because yesterday is now past.
Remember if you have faith, trouble won't last.

Don't think about tomorrow for it may never come.
Just remember to pray when you are feeling glum.

YESTERDAY
(continued)

"Let me hear from you, no matter the hour.
I, your Savior, have the listening and staying power."

"I don't get tired and I'm always there,
when you come to me in sincere prayer."

"Tribulations and strife are tape measures of your faith.
Hold on for Christ sake! He is your saving grace."

"Remember, I tell you your troubles won't last.
Your faith will rid you of them in a flash!

"*Do not follow where the path may lead. Go instead
where there is no path and leave a trail.*"

Ralph Waldo Emerson

CHAPTER 4

THE STRUGGLE

*"Since all great journeys start with a single step, you should probably
have on a cute pair of shoes."*
Author Unknown

MY DADDY MY MOMMY

Did you know my daddy done up and gone.
He just walked out, left mommy and us kids alone.

Told mommy he needed his space,
then moved on to some other place.

Never stopped to tell us kids goodbye.
Just flew the coupe like a bird in the sky.

Sometimes I wonder if he ever thought about us.
Too late to ask because he has bit the dust.
It seems all my life the subject of his leaving
was hush, hush.

Years went by before I knew my daddy lived in 'Chi' town.
A big Illinois city where unencumbered he could clown.

I thought to myself, that's okay,
if that's what he wanted to do!

Didn't know him, couldn't miss him, I guess I really didn't
care, because mommy was always there.

MY DADDY MY MOMMY
(continued)

This young woman at the age of twenty-eight,
nurtured seven kids without a break.

She saw that we kids had all the right stuff,
while without complaining she didn't have very much.

As adults us kids have supplied her material needs,
And our father divine continues to hear her pleas.

Mother, I love you in spite of misunderstandings we've had.
You've been a good mother and I'm glad.

I think of you often, and it hurts really bad
when I talk to you and sometimes you sound sad.

I wish you happiness every day of my life.
May God grant you peace as he takes away strife.

LOVE ALWAYS

"Faith is a choice to trust God even when the road ahead seems uncertain."

Dave Willis

JUST BLESSED

GOD blessed you with the most precious baby, **ME**, of
course, is there another?

GOD blessed me with incredible **YOU**, the earth's most
wonderful **MOTHER**!

Enjoy this special day; the cards, the gifts,
the flowers to you are dedicated;
to show how much you're loved, so favored and
appreciated!

I pray you're continuously blessed by **GOD**
for all the great things that you do;

I know that the world would be better if there were more
MOTHERS like **YOU**!

HAPPY MOTHER'S DAY

"Basically, there are two paths you can walk: faith or fear. It's impossible to simultaneously trust God and not trust God."

Dr. Charles Stanley

MISSING IN ACTION
IN CELEBRATION OF FATHER'S DAY

My Heavenly Father has always been near to monitor,
nurture, teach, protect, and provide for me.
He has led me down the curving paths of life, bracing me as
I stumbled along the way.

He has taught me to be fearless and to have confidence
when confronted with the chaos of the world.
with the chaos.
He has His hand on me!

You My Earthly Father: Missing In Action
Who Are You? Where Are You?
Why were you a stranger?
Someone I barely knew?
Why did you abandon me? Why?
What did I do?

But because I am a Child of God: I can truly say. . .
I STILL LOVE YOU and HAVE A WONDERFUL

FATHER'S DAY!

"Yours are the only shoes made to walk your journey."

Charles F. Glassman

PISSED!

What is on the mind of this new generation of parents?
Some are so twisted that they have chosen
to refer to their newborns as **'THEY-BIES'**!

What a disparaging term to call God's most precious gift.

Are they trying to protect themselves from the shock and
dismay that might occur when the child gets older
and chooses a same sex partner or identifies as transgender?

Don't let your child grow up confused about their gender
and wondering about their assigned genitalia?
The term 'Theybe' will only make them wonder
"Who Am I" and "What Am I!"

Biologically, humans were created male and female.
While gender dysphoria exists and
presents a variety of challenges,
it does not necessitate or validate a new human species.

I am not prejudiced, judgmental nor disrespectful of the
rights, values, opinions, and beliefs of others.
However, I think that even the LGBT community would be
offended if referred to as a 'They-be'!

PISSED!
(continued)

It is incredulous that parents would burden their children
with such a frivolous trend,
rather than tell them the truth and teach them to be resilient
to the harsh scrutiny that they are likely to face
in our ever-changing, chaotic world.

"Walk with me for a while, my friend – you in my shoes, I in yours – and then let us talk."

Richelle E. Goodrich

GOD, PATIENCE, PEACE

Pray to God for patience to ensure peace.
Patience prevents angry tirades.

Patience leaves the heart open to compassion and caring.
Patience allows one to see beyond the turmoil of the world.

Patience alleviates negativity.
Patience soothes the soul,
so that healing from emotional pain will occur.

Patience awakens the mind to perceive the Glory of God,
then one can experience peace within forever more.

The key to PATIENCE is prayer.
The key to PEACE is patience.

The key to it all is belief and faith in GOD!

CHAPTER 5

THE FIGHT

"Give a girl the right shoes and she can conquer the world."
Marilyn Monroe

DEVIL ANGEL
HEAVEN ANGEL

The Devil Angel, I never rest,
and I'm always trying to do my best
to administer a malicious and sinister test.

I am definitely there to cramp your style,
doing everything to remove your comfort
and pleasant smile.

I twist your tongue until it is as sharp as a dagger,
piercing the spirit of your sisters and brothers,
proclaiming it's okay to offend and kill others!

Attack, attack!
Every chance that I get,
hold grudges, carry baggage…oh well what the heck.
I don't need anyone to receive my paycheck.

Be carefree, think nothing but Me, Myself and I,
misery is the only company I need, and it's required!

I scream, holler, cuss, and put others down,
it is music to my ears, so I hang around.

DEVIL ANGEL HEAVEN ANGEL

(continued)

Thinking negative thoughts,
making sure people know that I am about to explode,
ready to deliver another deadly blow!

Doing everything to cause friends and loved ones to flee,
then I'll be filled with glee,
satisfied that your soul now belongs to me.

Hold on, hold on, not so fast Devil man,
the Heaven Angel, God's child, is taking a stand!

The ear of fervent prayer will hear and stomp you out,
then, I'll show you what Christianity is all about,
the reason why so many sing, dance and shout!

I'll pray that the tongue will be bridled
and patience restored,
and innocent mistakes will be politely ignored.

DEVIL ANGEL
HEAVEN ANGEL
(continued)

Rants and rage will be replaced by calm and sincere
discussion, honest opinions expressed without loud and
angry commotions.

Family, friends and foe will want to listen and hear ideas
and wisdom, spoken in peace with a quiet disposition.

A true, positive resolve and successful solution
I bring to all Christians anointed for the mission to help
carry out the Holy Commission.

The Heaven Angel will never let go!
Devil Angel, you will never claim a real Christian soul!

"Walking a mile in someone else's shoes isn't as much about the walk or the shoes; it's to be able to think like they think, feel what they feel, and understand why they are who and where they are. Every step is about empathy."

Toni Sorenson

LORD, LORD, LORD PLEASE FIX THIS MESS!

You, My Father, have provided me
with what I need to live a good life.
I thank you daily, morning, noon and night.

However, the devil seems to loom in the midst,
creeping about and causing strife.

He takes the most innocent statements,
twists and turns them into lies.
When he's called out on them of course he denies!

There's constant turmoil in my home,
the one you loaned me to call my own.

I pray Heavenly Father that you'll soon fix this mess.
Lord, lift this weight up off my chest!

AMEN

"My momma always said there's an awful lot you can tell about a person by their shoes."

Forrest Gump

SIMPLY PUT

Today, Lord, I would just like to have a pleasant
conversation with those who surround me.

Simply put, the subject does not have to be that deep.
The weather, the breeze, as it moves the leaves on the trees;
the animals, the menu or attire.

Any one of these topics could upstage rage,
dispel strife, reduce stress,
and at best allow the mind to rest.

Simply put, just spend a little down time
by focusing on the pleasantries in life.

Connecting with God by praying to receive peace and
Stomp the Devil Out!

*"Give a girl the right shoes and she can
conquer the world."*

Marilyn Monroe

DON'T WORRY

Don't worry about failure, however, do be concerned.
Concern will motivate you to listen and learn.

Don't worry about failure. Just pray for success,
and in everything you do make the effort your best!

Hold your head up high. Look challenge in the eye.
Then reach, yes reach, reach for the sky.

Let God be the head of your life. Let Him have control.
Don't worry about failure. Focus on your goal!

Trust Christ, your Great Helper, who is very much alive.
He knows all about you and walks by your side.

Don't worry about failure. Your dreams will be realized,
and everything you need, He will provide!

*"Do not be anxious about anything, but in every situation, by prayer
and petition, with thanksgiving, present your requests to God. And
the peace of God, which transcends all understanding, will guard your
hearts and your minds in Christ Jesus."*
Philippians 4:6-7 NIV

OH LORD,
HEAR A SINNER'S PRAYER

Dear Lord, hear my prayer.

I come to you on bended knee,
my hands raised to give you praise.

I know you know my needs,
yet I pray today that you will remove despair...
plant within my soul, hope, the tiny but powerful seeds.

Help me Lord to endure the tribulations of the land,
while I hold on humbly with trembling hands.

I want to draw strength from you through Jesus Christ,
who died that I may have everlasting life.

My desires, oh Lord, are many; to be obedient, forgiving,
and drenched in integrity.
Lord, dredge up a storm. Rain down on me.

OH LORD,
HEAR A SINNER'S PRAYER
(continued)

Last and most importantly, I ask oh Lord,
that you will forgive my sins…
anoint me Lord, that I may be a blessing to strangers,
family, and friends.

Lord, I'll stand.
I know your love for me is great!
An answer to my prayer, I patiently await.

*"I've worn lots of shoes. I bet if I think about it really
hard I could remember my first pair of shoes."*

Forrest Gump

HE ANSWERS PRAYER

If only you trust Him, have faith, and never doubt.
Oh yes, He will work everything out!

In fervent submission on your bended knees,
call on the Heavenly Father, please!

Hope is inevitable you will find,
when you talk to the Master,
He is your Father divine.

His spirit is with you everywhere.
Believe, believe, don't despair.

God loves His children, and He answers prayer.
Call Him morning, noon, or night, in the name of Jesus.
He'll make everything right.

He hears the sinners as well as the Christian prayer.
No matter what, He's always there.

Speak to Him. Speak to Him.
He answers prayer.

CHAPTER 6

THE RESTORATION

"My momma always said there's an awful lot you can tell about a person by their shoes. Where they going...where they been."
Forrest Gump

WHO ARE WE

We are but a speck in the sea of God's love,
allowed by His amazing grace
to tread the waters of the world daily to stay afloat.

Powerless to make it on our own,
He is our sustainer!
We are the putty in His hands
to be molded and used as He sees fit.

Prayer is our connection to God.
Praise Him and give Him the glory, Always!

I know you are God's child,
who knows all about praying, and God answers prayer.

When asked, He will touch you with His healing hand,
working with you, and walking with you on your journey.

It is my prayer as I lift you up to our Savior
that you soon will be made whole, comfortable,
and at peace.

*"If you don't think shoes are important, just ask
Cinderella and Dorothy."*

Author Unknown

PEACE WITHIN

Looking out the window at a clear beautiful sky.
I think, oh Lord, how glad I am to be alive.
Bountifully blessed to breathe your breath, I sigh.

Peace is not upon earth, but I have peace within.

My prayer is oh Lord, the peace I have within
will come out and be a beacon of light
to someone without a friend.

That they too may be bountifully blessed
to breathe your breath
and experience the peace within.

"Since all great journeys start with a single step, you should probably have on a cute pair of shoes."

Author Unknown

THE MAN IN MY LIFE

Immortal is the man in my life.
Trusting Him protects me from strife.

He's wonderful, He's marvelous; and brings me joy.
I adore Him, I adore Him. I'm not being coy.

The things I want, He says, "just
ask and to you they shall be given".
He's real, He's real, well and living.

Immortal is the man in my life,
He's so good to me.
I love Him and worship Him
in prayer on bended knees.

I love Him, I love Him, oh can't you see?
I love Him, I love Him, and He loves me.

He died for my sins on Calvary.

"It doesn't matter how great your shoes are if you don't accomplish anything in them."

Martina Boone, Compulsion

GOD, YOU ARE MY SUNSHINE

God, you are my sunshine,
there is something magnificent
in each of your rays.

You awaken me each morning
and start my day.

Your solar power ignites my soul,
spiritually fueling the flesh,
you are in control.

As I orbit the earth running the race,
I encounter many narrow paths,
all littered with stumbling blocks,
strategically placed.

Satan appears now and again
to tempt me as he beckons.
It's okay to follow me he reckons.

GOD, YOU ARE MY SUNSHINE
(continued)

Trudging along tired and weary,
again I hear Satan's call.

God, I pray you activate my booster
lest I fall.

You answered Lord,
and with confidence I looked to the sky.

As light turned to darkness, I saw the moon.
I envisioned your face all aglow.
Mirrored by the stars not once but tenfold.

Running, running, I keep running Lord,
as your face lights up the night.
Knowing salvation is the trophy promised
at the end of my plight.

Satan, Satan, it is you I abhor.
God, you are my sunshine and
so much more.
It is you I adore.

"Sometimes the best thing to do is stop, breathe and focus on the positive. If that doesn't work, try a new pair of shoes."

Author Unknown

LOVE IS

Today is the day that I want to say,
God is Love
and emotion shown from heaven above.

In the midst of joy and adversity, the spirit of love rains
down on thee with this in mind.

I surely pray
you'll celebrate the holiday in a Christian way.

Peace and Goodwill.

"Mama said they'd take me anywhere...she said they was my magic shoes."

Forrest Gump

LONG ARMS OF LOVE

Reach out, reach out, long arms of love –
encircle mankind and all humanity.

Encircle that which touches you each day,
in some bold, discreet, or uncanny way.

The need is there to feel an embrace,
by all you see, no matter what the case.

Love is listed among the hierarchy of needs.
Plant it, pollinize it like any seed.

With nurturing care, it will bud;
like fingers attached to the hands,
that extends from your long arms of love,
that surrounds our being and fits like a glove.

RECIPE FOR EVERLASTING LIFE

Start with a tribulation,
Add a sea of blessing, a wave of grace and mercy
from the Great I Am.

Mix with faith, love, and charity, and
belief in the trinity.

Stir in the promise of salvation;
recognizing God is the beginning and the end time
is of essence!

When you have asked for forgiveness of your sins
and live according to His word,
the recipe is complete,
and your soul shall rise.

BRENDA'S PRAYER

Dear Lord, I woke up this morning
because you touched me with your finger of love.
You watched over me all night from heaven above.

You let no harm come to me as I slept and slumbered,
peacefully I rested in your safe arms of comfort.

I give you all the glory and praise!
Oh Lord, you never cease to amaze!
As I live through this glorious day, let me be mindful of all
of the wonderful things you have made.

I will be compassionate and caring to others,
seeking to love all my sisters and brothers.

I just want to be pleasing in your sight.
Lord, I'm trying to do what is right!

AMEN

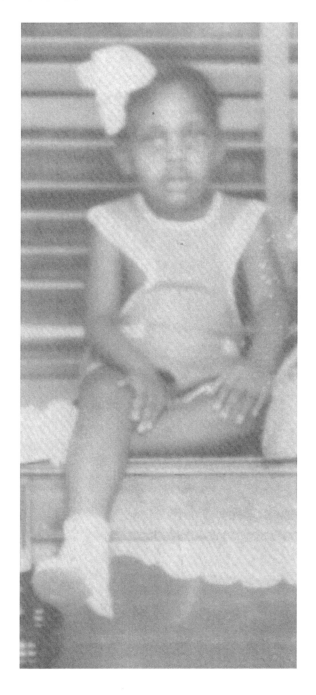

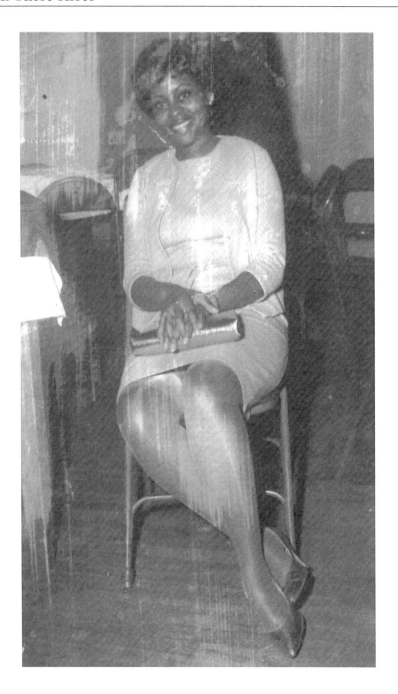

"*Sometimes, the best thing you can do is stop, breathe and focus on the positive. And if that doesn't work, try a new pair of shoes.*"

Author Unknown

"It doesn't matter how great your shoes are
if you don't accomplish anything in them."
Martina Boone, Compulsion

About The Author

Brenda Ruth Stevenson's story is one of resilience, dedication, and love. Born on October 13, 1939, in St. Louis, Missouri, Brenda's early years were shaped by her godmother, Lucille Owens. Growing up as the fourth of seven siblings, Brenda finished high school at Douglas High School in Columbia, Missouri, before returning to her hometown of St. Louis.

Brenda pursued a career in healthcare and quickly became a force to be reckoned with. Starting as an LPN, she worked her way up to becoming a registered nurse, and even earned a master's degree in nursing administration – a feat that she remains incredibly proud of to this day. All the while, Brenda raised three daughters on her own and inspired them to pursue their own academic and professional goals despite life's challenges.

Described as an empathic, generous and caring individual, Brenda enjoyed writing and sewing before her eyesight began to worsen. She was also a proud owner of a ladies' boutique, reflecting her passion for fashion and love of shoes. After retiring, Brenda moved to Atlanta, Georgia, where she resides today.

Brenda's journey is a testament to the power of determination and the importance of family. Her example has inspired many, and her legacy will continue to inspire for generations to come.

Contact The Author